D0272436

History Through Poetry
World War II

Reg Grant

HODDER
Wayland

an imprint of Hodder Children's Books

Kill

920–44)

lass appears
ing to die.
out in ways
ts of his.
e: I cry
iar, hears

of dust
rcery
mused
sed
acancy.
st.

**Canary in a
Air-Raid**

Myfanwy Haycock (19

All suddenly your tin
Among the pand
Threading their gia
Obstinately w

So clear y
Above t
Spilling

History Through Poetry
Tudors
Victorians
World War I
World War II

Commissioning Editor: Alex Woolf
Editor: Jonathan Ingoldby
Designer: Simon Borrough
Cover Concept: Peta Morey

Published in Great Britain in 2001 by Hodder Wayland, an imprint of Hodder Children's Books
This edition reprinted in 2002
© Copyright 2001 Hodder Wayland

All rights reserved. No part of this publication may be reproduced, stored in a retrieval system, or transmitted, in any form or by any means without the prior written permission of the publisher, nor be otherwise circulated in any form of binding or cover other than that in which it is published and without a similar condition being imposed on the subsequent publisher.

British Library Cataloguing in Publication Data
Grant, Reg 1954–
    World War II. – (History Through Poetry)
    1. English poetry – 20th century – Juvenile literature
    2. World War, 1939–1945 – Juvenile literature
    I.Title
    940.5'3

ISBN 0 7502 3591 8

Printed in Hong Kong by Wing King Tong

Hodder Children's Books
A division of Hodder Headline Limited
338 Euston Road, London, NW1 3BH

Cover and Decorative Pictures:
The cover shows an army officer's cap, World War II medals, a standard-issue stationery wallet with envelopes, a pencil with cap made from a bullet, and a World War II ammunition box (all courtesy of the Imperial War Museum); a photograph of a wireless operator (courtesy of Zul Mukhida); a regimental badge from Burma (courtesy of Simon Borrough). The pictures that appear on the left-hand pages of the book are Sam Browne belt and officer's revolver (p. 4); gas mask (p. 6); scarf decorated with 'Walls Have Ears' cartoon (p. 8); evacuee's knapsack (p. 10); stationery wallet and envelopes (p. 12); 8th Army bookends (p. 14); tankard made from a shell-case (p. 16); survival rations (p. 18); World War II medals (p. 20); regimental badge (p. 22); officer's cap (p. 24); shelter lamp (p. 26) (all courtesy of the Imperial War Museum unless otherwise stated). All objects date from the period.

Special thanks are due to Allan Jefferies, Department of Exhibits and Firearms, Imperial War Museum.

Picture Acknowledgements
The publishers would like to thank the following for permission to reproduce their pictures: Aberdeen Press and Journal/Hodder Wayland Picture Library 9 (bottom), 25 (bottom); Hulton Getty 5 (bottom); Imperial War Museum/ Hodder Wayland Picture Library 5 (bottom), 7 (bottom), 11 (bottom), 13 (bottom); Peter Newark's Military Pictures 7 (top), 9 (top), 11 (top), 17 (top), 19 (left), 21 (right), 27 (top), 29 (bottom); Popperfoto 13 (top), 15 (bottom), 19 (right), 21 (left), 23, 27 (bottom), 29 (top); Topham Picturepoint 15 (top), 17 (bottom), 25 (top).

Poetry Acknowledgements
The publishers are grateful to the following for permission to reproduce copyright material:

Arthur Stockwell Ltd (Doris Burton, 'Children of the War'); R.N. Currey ('Unseen Fire'); Faber & Faber Ltd (Keith Douglas, 'How to Kill', from *Complete Poems*); David Higham Associates (Louis MacNeice, 'Swing Song' from *Collected Poems*, published by Faber & Faber); Macmillan Publishers Ltd (Wilfrid Wilson Gibson, 'When the Plane Dived'); Methuen Publishing Ltd (Bertolt Brecht, 'To the German Soldiers in the East', trans. John Willet, from *Bertolt Brecht: Poems 1913–1956*; Michael Riviere, 'Oflag Night Piece', from *The Terrible Rain: The War Poets 1939–45*, ed. Brian Gardner); Oxford University Press (Henry Reed, 'Naming of Parts' from *Lessons of the War*, a sequence of five poems © The Executor of Henry Reed's Estate 1946, 1947, 1970 and 1991, reprinted from *Henry Reed: Collected Poems*, ed. Jon Stallworthy 1991); Peters Fraser & Dunlop Group Limited (Roger McGough, 'Snipers', from *Watchwords*, reprinted by permission of PFD on behalf of Roger McGough); Weidenfeld & Nicholson (Marc Kaminsky, 'Every Month: The Ten-Year-Old Girl'); Wynn Williams and Gwladys Haycock (Myfanwy Haycock, 'Canary in an Air-Raid').

Every effort has been made to trace the copyright holders of material reproduced in this book. Any rights not acknowledged here will be acknowledged in subsequent printings if notice is given to the publisher.

CONTENTS

Naming of Parts

Henry Reed (1914–86)

✿

Today we have naming of parts. Yesterday,
We had daily cleaning. And tomorrow morning,
We shall have what to do after firing. But today,
Today we have naming of parts. Japonica
Glistens like coral in all of the neighbouring
gardens
And today we have naming of parts.

✿

This is the lower sling swivel. And this
Is the upper sling swivel, whose use you will see
When you are given your slings. And this is the
piling swivel,
Which in your case you have not got. The
branches
Hold in the gardens their silent, eloquent
gestures,
Which in our case we have not got.

(c.1941)

naming of parts
Learning the names of the different parts of a rifle.

Japonica
A beautiful flowering plant.

sling swivel, piling swivel
Parts of a rifle.

eloquent
Expressive.

The poet is one of a group of conscripts being taught about their rifles in the open air on a fine spring day. There are two different voices in the poem. The instructor speaks the first four lines (almost) in each verse. The last two-and-a-bit lines are the poet talking to himself. He is distracted from the boring lesson by the nearby gardens. The fact that the soldiers did not have some parts of a rifle was common early in the war – there was not enough proper equipment to go round.

A soldier says farewell to his family.

POET'S CORNER

Henry Reed was a journalist and writer before he was called up for service in the army in 1941. He didn't stay in the army for long, but soon transferred to a desk job at the Foreign Office. To judge by this poem, that must have come as a great relief to him!

Most of the men who fought in World War II were not professional soldiers. They were 'conscripts' – people from all walks of life forced to join the armed forces whether they liked it or not. In Britain, any man between the ages of 18 and 41 could be 'called up' for military service. Only those with important jobs, such as skilled workers, were let off.

Being introduced to a rifle.

The war began in September 1939. By the following Christmas, over a million young men had been rushed into uniform. Taken away from family and friends, their first experience of army life was mostly boring and depressing. In training camps they were bullied all day long by corporals and sergeant-majors as they learned to march and handle weapons.

Canary in an Air-Raid

Myfanwy Haycock (1913–63)

❀

All suddenly your tiny voice rang shrill
Among the pandemonium of guns,
Threading their giant thunderstorm of sound
Obstinately with little trills and runs.

❀

So clear you sang, so daringly and clear
Above those angry guns' incessant rage,
Spilling brave notes through all the shuddering
house
In cascades from your flimsy prison-cage.

❀

And we, who crouched beneath the basement
stairs
While every thud seemed ominous with doom
And unbreathed fear, grew suddenly ashamed
To hear your singing in an upper room.

(1944)

air-raid
Attack by enemy aircraft dropping bombs.

pandemonium
Uproar; loud noise and confusion.

trills and runs
Musical notes.

cascades
Falling streams; in this case, of birdsong.

ominous
As if disaster was on the way.

Air raids were a terrifying experience for people on the ground, never sure whether the next bomb was going to fall on top of their house or shelter. In this poem, bombs are falling and all the people in a house have gone to hide under the stairs in the basement – the safest place they can find. They have not taken their pet canary with them. While they tremble with fear as the house is shaken by explosions and the roar of the anti-aircraft guns fills the night, they hear the canary begin to sing. It makes them feel ashamed of their fear.

Uuring the winter of 1940–41, London was heavily bombed by the German air force, the Luftwaffe. This is known as the 'Blitz'. Other cities in Britain were also 'blitzed', including Coventry, Liverpool, Plymouth and Glasgow.

POET'S CORNER

Born near Pontypool, in Monmouthshire, Myfanwy Haycock spent the early years of the war in Cardiff, where her jobs included a spell in a munitions factory. During this time Cardiff was bombed by the Germans. Myfanwy Haycock never became a famous poet, but her poems were published in newspapers and magazines, and she several times read her verse on television.

Left: Firefighters tackle a blazing warehouse after a German bombing raid.

The bombers mostly came by night. To make it difficult for them to find their targets, street lights were switched off and windows were covered so that no light showed outside – this was called the 'blackout'. As the bombers approached, an air-raid warning went off. Some people hurried to concrete shelters. Others simply hid under the stairs in their homes. In London, thousands slept on underground station platforms as bombs exploded overhead.

Civilians shelter from an air raid in a London Underground tube station.

Swing-Song

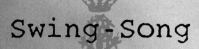

Louis MacNeice (1907–63)

❀

I'm only a wartime working girl,
The machine-shop makes me deaf,
I have no prospects after the war
And my young man is in the RAF
K for Kitty calling P for Prue...
Bomb Doors Open...
Over to You.

❀

Night after night as he passes by
I wonder what he's gone to bomb
And I fancy in the jabber of the mad machines
That I hear him talking on the intercomm.
K for Kitty calling P for Prue...
Bomb Doors Open...
Over to You.

(1942)

machine-shop
A factory with heavy machinery.

no prospects
No chance of a good job or money.

RAF
Royal Air Force.

jabber
Senseless talk.

intercomm
Now usually spelt 'intercom', an internal radio or telephone system, for example on an aircraft.

In this excerpt, a young woman working a night-shift in a factory thinks about her boyfriend, who is flying night-time bombing missions over Germany. She imagines that she can hear the bomber crew talking to one another over their target, using a code made up of women's names. She probably feels lonely and jealous, left behind in her deafeningly noisy factory. She certainly has a low opinion of herself – 'only a wartime working girl'. In the rhythm of the poem, the poet has tried to get the feel of the 'swing' music (big-band jazz) that was popular at the time.

As men went off to fight, women were forced to take over many of the jobs they left behind. Factories making guns, tanks and bombs employed women workers, while thousands were sent to work on farms as part of the 'Land Army'. There were also women's branches of the armed forces, although women were not sent into battle. Some women welcomed the new experiences that the war brought them. But the jobs they had to do were often hard and unrewarding.

With their husbands away at the war, mothers had to bring up families on their own in difficult wartime conditions. Shortages of food and other essentials made daily life a constant struggle. And women had to cope with worry about loved ones – boyfriends, sons or husbands – who might be killed in action any day.

WOMEN OF BRITAIN
COME INTO THE FACTORIES

ASK AT ANY EMPLOYMENT EXCHANGE FOR ADVICE AND FULL DETAILS

A poster encouraging women to work in the munitions factories.

POET'S CORNER

Louis MacNeice was born in Northern Ireland. He published his first book of poems in 1929, when he was still a student at Oxford University. By the time the war broke out, he was one of the best-known poets of his day. MacNiece worked for BBC radio in London during the war.

A force to be reckoned with! Women's Land Army girls on parade in February 1941.

Children of War

Doris Burton

❁

We gaze at the yellow sands.
They tell us
Once children made castles and forts,
And dug deep holes with their spades,
Fetched water in bright coloured pails,
Whilst they laughed and shouted and ran.
They bathed in that shimmering sea,
Sailed boats, and caught tiny crabs on the rocks.
What joy!

❁

But for us
There are coils of rusty barbed wire,
And spiked iron guards.
There are mines — they blew up a dog!
Oh, yes, it was killed quite dead.
So we may not go to the shore.
We are children of war!

(c.1940)

pails
Buckets.

spiked iron guards
Large metal obstacles.

During the war, British children missed out on many normal peacetime treats – including trips to the seaside. Because of the fear that Britain might be invaded from the sea, many beaches were treated like the front line in a battle zone. Mines were buried under the sand and the edge of the sea was lined with barbed wire and iron and concrete obstacles. In this poem, the sight of a sandy beach reminds the poet of the ordinary pleasures of pre-war life. Now the seaside is a place of danger and definitely out of bounds.

LEAVE THIS TO US
SONNY—<u>YOU</u> OUGHT
TO BE OUT OF LONDON

MINISTRY OF HEALTH EVACUATION SCHEME

A poster from 1942 advertising the evacuation scheme.

POET'S CORNER

Born in Essex, Doris Burton was a devout Catholic. She was one of many thousands of people who turned to writing poetry as a way of expressing their experience of the war. She never became well-known for her writing.

For hundreds of thousands of British children, the first experience of the war was 'evacuation'. Because of a fear that cities would be bombed flat, children were sent to live in the countryside. For many poor children from city slums, it was their first sight of real cows and fields. When the expected destruction of cities failed to happen early in the war, many evacuees returned home and endured the bombing with their families.

Whether evacuated or not, children's lives were disrupted. They often had long periods off school, especially when school buildings were damaged by bombs, and their education suffered. However, despite shortages – bananas were a forgotten dream – rationing ensured that they generally had enough nourishing food to eat.

Evacuees of various ages, shown with their gas-masks in cardboard boxes.

OCCUPATION AND HOLOCAUST

Last Supper

Luba Krugman Gurdus (1914–)

❁

*Soup simmers quietly
And it's hard to bear
That this is the last supper
We will ever share*

❁

*Early in the morning
We'll surely be moved
To the Collection Center
With the local Jews*

❁

*Then we will be pushed
To waiting cattle cars
And wild Nazi shouts
Will stifle babies' cries*

❁

*I finished my peasoup
And covered the moist eyes
This is our last supper
And our last goodbye...*

(c.1943)

cattle cars
Railway wagons intended for transporting animals.

Nazi
The Nazi (National Socialist) party ruled Germany during the war.

moist eyes
Her eyes are wet with tears.

After Germany invaded Poland at the start of the war, the Nazi authorities made all Jewish people there live in 'ghettos' – separate areas of towns. This poem was written by a woman in a ghetto. Her family have been ordered to go, with their few possessions, to an assembly point. She knows that they will be taken by train, in hideous conditions, to a camp where they will probably be killed. This is why it is their 'last supper'. She covers her eyes because she does not want the young ones to see how upset she is.

Children in the Warsaw Ghetto, 1942. In January of that year 90 children in the Ghetto died of starvation.

P O E T ' S C O R N E R

Luba Krugman Gurdus is a Jewish woman who was born in Poland. In the Warsaw Ghetto she wrote poems in her diary. She survived the Holocaust and now lives in the United States.

From 1940 to 1945 a large part of Europe was occupied by German troops. Life for people under Nazi rule was very hard. Food and fuel were in very short supply – the Germans took most of what little there was. Resistance movements were formed to fight a secret war against the German occupation by, for example, blowing up trains or shooting soldiers. The Nazis carried out reprisals against local people, sometimes destroying whole villages.

The people who suffered worst under Nazi rule were the Jews. German dictator Adolf Hitler and his Nazi followers hated Jewish people and decided to kill them all – men, women and children. Millions of Jews were rounded up and sent to camps in German-occupied Poland, where most of them were gassed to death. This is called the Holocaust.

Victims in a Nazi camp, photographed immediately after the defeat of Germany.

DEATH IN THE DESERT

How to Kill

Keith Douglas (1920–44)

❀

Now in my dial of glass appears
the soldier who is going to die.
He smiles, and moves about in ways
his mother knows, habits of his.
The wires touch his face: I cry
NOW. Death, like a familiar, hears

❀

and look, has made a man of dust
of a man of flesh. This sorcery
I do. Being damned, I am amused
to see the centre of love diffused
and the waves of love travel into vacancy.
How easy it is to make a ghost.

(1943)

dial of glass
A sight on a gun, used to help aim.

wires
The aiming lines on the gun-sight.

familiar
A spirit who carries out the commands of a witch or wizard.

sorcery
Magic.

diffused
Spread in all directions.

vacancy
Emptiness.

In a war, people who would normally never harm anyone have to kill fellow human beings. This poem tries to describe what it is like to kill someone. The poet doesn't hate the enemy soldier he has in his gun-sight. He can see that his victim is just an ordinary person, with a mother who loves him and his own little habits. Killing is like evil magic, that turns a living man into lifeless dust. The poet sees himself as 'damned', an evil creature who destroys the love at the heart of every human being. What strikes him in the end is how easy it is to kill.

Deat

De

Eighth Army troops capture a German tank.

The war took soldiers to many exotic parts of the world, including the deserts of North Africa. In these wide open spaces, British and German tanks fought a war of swift movement. Conditions in the desert were harsh, with a lack of water, heat by day and cold by night, and blinding sandstorms. But to many people it seemed that the desert war was what warfare should really be like, with soldiers fighting bravely in clear-cut battles and treating their enemies with old-fashioned chivalry. As in all war, however, death and suffering were the end result.

German General Erwin Rommel's Afrika Korps was a formidable enemy, but the Allies – chiefly Britain and its Commonwealth, and the United States – eventually won the war in the desert. They then used North Africa as a base from which to invade Italy in 1943.

POET'S CORNER

Keith Douglas was a tank commander in the British army and fought in the desert war, including the famous battle of Alamein in 1942. He was only 24 years old when he was killed in action in Normandy, three days after the 1944 D-Day landings. Douglas was one of the finest poets of World War II.

Erwin Rommel, commander of the German army in North Africa, photographed after the fall of Tobruk.

When the Plane Dived

Wilfrid Gibson (1878–1962)

✺

When the plane dived and the machine-gun spattered

The deck, in his numb clutch the tugging wheel

Bucked madly as he strove to keep the keel

Zig-zagging through the steep and choppy sea —

To keep zig-zagging, that was all that mattered...

To keep the ship zig-zagging endlessly,

Dodging that diving devil. Now again

The bullets spattered like a squall of rain

About him; and again with a desperate grip

He tugged, to port the helm ...to keep the ship

Zig-zagging... zig-zagging through eternity;

To keep the ship...A sudden scalding pain

Shot through his shoulder and the whole sky shattered

About him in red fire; and yet his grip

Tightened upon the wheel...To keep the ship...

Zig... zig... zig-zagging, that was all that mattered.

(1943)

This poem celebrates the heroism of an ordinary sailor doing his duty. Steering a ship which is under air attack, he has to keep zig-zagging to make the ship a difficult target for the plane's guns. This takes a lot of physical effort as well as bravery – the wheel 'bucks' like a horse trying to throw off its rider as the rough waves of 'the steep and choppy sea' batter the ship. Eventually the sailor is hit by a bullet in the shoulder, but his dedication to duty is unbroken and he keeps on steering.

bucked
Jumped up and down.

keel
Bottom of a ship.

to port the helm
Steering to the left (port) side using the helm: the tiller or wheel which controls a ship's rudder.

In World War II, warships could no longer operate without aircraft to defend them against enemy air attack. Aircraft carriers provided air cover for fleets at sea, and became a major attack force. It was a strike by Japanese naval aircraft against the American fleet at Pearl Harbor that brought the United States into the war in December 1941.

Britain was especially dependent on the bravery of its seamen. German submarines, or U-boats, posed a major threat to Britain's survival. Food and fuel had to be imported by sea. Convoys of merchant ships crossed the Atlantic, protected by destroyers but hunted by 'wolf packs' of submarines. The U-boats began to sink so many merchant ships that it seemed Britain might be starved into submission. Eventually the U-boat menace was overcome, but it was a close-run thing.

A poster expressing gratitude for the all-important role played by the merchant navy in getting supplies across the Atlantic.

POET'S CORNER

Wilfrid Gibson made his reputation as a poet before World War I. He was far too old to fight in World War II. Perhaps this is why he expressed the heroism of warfare in a straightforward way. Poets who actually took part in the war took a more cynical and complicated view of it.

A convoy of merchant ships as seen from the deck of the escort ship, 1940.

To the German Soldiers in the East

Bertolt Brecht (1896–1955)

❁

Brothers, if I were with you —
Were one of you out there in the eastern
snowfields
One of the thousands of you amid the iron
chariots —
I would say as you say: Surely
There must be a road leading home.

❁

On the map in the schoolboy's atlas
The road to Smolensk is no bigger
Than the Führer's little finger, but
In the snowfields it is further
Very far, too far.

❁

The snow will not last for ever, just till
springtime.
But men will not last for ever either. Springtime
Will be too long.

(c.1943)

eastern snowfields
The snowy winter countryside of Russia.

iron chariots
Tanks.

Smolensk
A city in western Russia, on the soldiers' way home to Germany.

the Führer
The German dictator, Adolf Hitler.

This poem is addressed to German soldiers who are retreating across Russia in winter. In the extract, the poet speaks as a fellow German who could easily have been 'one of you out there'. He imagines the soldiers remembering how small the vast wastes of Russia looked on the maps they saw at school. By mentioning 'the Führer's little finger' he implies that Hitler himself, in his grandiose dreams of conquest, had fatally underestimated the size of the country he invaded. The poet believes that the soldiers will not survive the winter – as many thousands in fact did not.

In 1941 Germany invaded the Soviet Union. Ruled by the communist dictator Joseph Stalin, the Soviet Union covered a vast area including Russia, Belorus and Ukraine. The Germans soon reached the outskirts of Stalin's capital, Moscow, but they were eventually defeated by the harshness of the Russian winter, the huge distances they had to cover, and the skill and bravery of Soviet soldiers.

Famous poet and playwright Bertolt Brecht was a German who opposed Hitler. In 1933, when Hitler took power, Brecht fled into exile and spent most of the war in the United States. During the war he was in the painful position of wishing for the defeat of his own country. He returned to Germany after the war, running a theatre company in communist East Berlin.

Right: Snow-camouflaged Red Army infantry, supported by artillery fire, assault German positions near Leningrad, November 1942.

Stalingrad, 1942, *by Boris Ugarov: an artist's impression of Russian troops defending the city against the Germans.*

The war on the Eastern Front was exceptionally brutal. Germany's Nazi rulers regarded Russians and other Slavs as sub-human peoples to be mercilessly exploited or killed. Stalin was almost equally ruthless in the defence of his country. There were massive casualties in great tank battles and in the epic struggle for the city of Stalingrad. The Soviet army drove the Germans back and eventually invaded Germany. Soviet troops fought their way into the German capital, Berlin, in May 1945.

The Battle

Louis Simpson (1923–)

❁

Helmet and rifle, pack and overcoat
Marched through a forest. Somewhere up ahead
Guns thudded. Like the circle of a throat
The night on every side was turning red.

❁

They halted and they dug. They sank like moles
Into the clammy earth between the trees.
And soon the sentries, standing in their holes,
Felt the first snow. Their feet began to freeze.

❁

At dawn the first shell landed with a crack.
Then shells and bullets swept the icy woods.
This lasted many days. The snow was black.
The corpses stiffened in their scarlet hoods.

(c.1952)

clammy
Sticky.

scarlet hoods
Their heads are covered
with blood.

This poem is based on the writer's memory of the battle of Bastogne, when American troops fought the Germans in the winter of 1944–45. The soldiers in the poem have become faceless, without individuality. They are described as nothing but their uniforms and equipment. They do no active fighting – their role is to be shot at and to freeze. Writing in short sentences, the poet deliberately makes no comment and expresses no feeling. He said his aim was 'to show the war exactly, as though I were painting a landscape...'

The war brought more than 3 million American soldiers and airmen across the Atlantic to fight against the Nazis in Europe. Most of the 'GIs' (an abbreviation of 'general' or 'government' 'issue') spent some time at bases in Britain. Their presence had a great impact on local people – especially women. The GIs had money in their pockets and luxuries to offer around, such as nylon stockings and chocolate bars. British people jokingly complained that the 'Yanks' were 'overpaid, oversexed, and over here'.

Like British soldiers, the GIs were almost all conscripts. Few had seen action before D-Day – the seaborne invasion of Normandy in June 1944. It was a brutal baptism of fire which many did not survive. The US army was the dominant force in the fighting over the following year that brought the liberation of France, Belgium and the Netherlands, and the eventual defeat of Germany in the West.

POET'S CORNER

Born in Jamaica, Louis Simpson emigrated to the United States when he was 17. He joined the US army in 1943 and fought in Europe, surviving a wound and frostbite. After the war he had a nervous breakdown. As part of his recovery, he began writing poems based on his memories of the war, trying to describe 'the truth of what it had been like to be an American infantry soldier'.

Left: 6 June 1944: the D-Day landings. American troops wade onto the beaches in Northern France.

Above: The cover of the army magazine Yank Weekly, *23 July 1944, after the liberation of Paris. The photo shows a French girl helping GIs with their French.*

Snipers

Roger McGough (1937–)

When I was kneehigh to a tabletop,
Uncle Tom came home from Burma.
He was the youngest of seven brothers
so the street borrowed extra bunting
and whitewashed him a welcome.

All the relations made the pilgrimage,
including us, laughed, sang, made a fuss.
He was as brown as a chairleg,
drank tea out of a white mug the size of my
head,
and said next to nowt.

But every few minutes he would scan
the ceiling nervously, hands begin to shake.
'For snipers,' everyone later agreed,
'A difficult habit to break.'

(1968)

bunting
Flags.

whitewashed him a welcome
Gave buildings a coat of whitewash to smarten them up for his homecoming.

nowt
Nothing.

When soldiers returned from the war, many of them were shattered by their experiences. This was especially true of those who had fought in the jungles of Burma. In this poem, we see the respect paid to a returned soldier and how awesome he seemed to a small boy. But while the welcoming family laugh and sing, he is silent and trembling, still expecting snipers to fire at him from the branches of jungle trees. The family try to understand him, but perhaps they don't try very hard – the use of the word 'whitewashed' suggests that they might want to cover up Uncle Tom's real experience of the war.

Allied troops crossing a river in Burma.

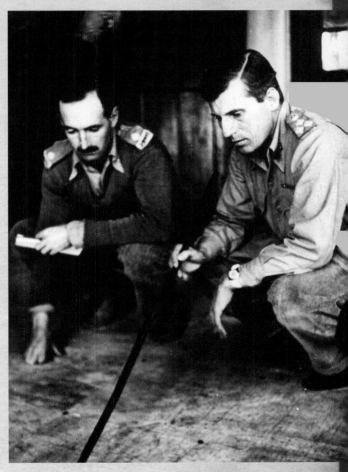

POET'S CORNER

Roger McGough was born in Liverpool in 1937. He became well-known in the 1960s as one of the 'Liverpool poets' – at a time when the Beatles had made the city trendy. He has written a number of poems based on memories of his wartime childhood.

In late 1941 and early 1942, Japanese forces took over much of the Pacific Ocean and South-East Asia. For the next three years, the United States and Britain fought to recapture these areas, including the jungles of Burma.

There was no scarier place for fighting than the jungle. It was hot, humid and full of dangerous creatures. The soldiers advanced by following narrow tracks made by wild animals. They carried only a small amount of food with them, often surviving on a diet of rice and tea. The Japanese soldiers were a fearsome enemy, moving silently and attacking with deadly suddenness. Dedicated to the service of their emperor, they were unwilling to surrender even when facing certain death. Nevertheless, most of Burma was in Allied hands by May 1945.

Orde Wingate, Commander of the 77th Indian Brigade in Burma, discusses strategy.

PRISONERS OF WAR

Oflag Night Piece

Michael Riviere (1919–)

❀

There, where the swifts flicker along the wall
And the last light catches — there in the high
schloss
(How the town grows dark) all's made
impregnable:
They bless each window with a double cross
Of iron; weave close banks of wire and train
Machine guns down them; and look — at the first
star
Floodlight the startled darkness back again...
All for three hundred prisoners of war.
Yet now past them and the watch they keep,
Unheard, invisible, in ones and pairs,
In groups, in companies — alarms are dumb,
A sentry loiters, a blind searchlight stares —
Unchallenged as their memories of home
The vanishing prisoners escape to sleep.

(1944)

Oflag
Prisoner-of-war camp.

swifts
Fast-flying birds.

schloss
German for 'castle'.

impregnable
Something that can't be broken into, or out of.

train
Aim.

This poem was written by a British prisoner of war in a German castle, Colditz. It is evening. The castle's windows have crossed iron bars on them and the castle is surrounded by barbed wire and machine-guns to prevent escape. Floodlights come on as soon as it is dark. But despite all these precautions, the prisoners are still able to escape – inside their heads. Their memories and their dreams are free, and there is nothing their captors can do about it.

Millions of soldiers of all nationalities were captured by their enemies at some stage during the war. They had the experience of being 'prisoners of war', or POWs – sometimes for four or five years. There were rules laid down to guarantee decent treatment for prisoners. For example, all prisoners were supposed to be allowed to receive food parcels and mail via the Red Cross. Officers were not supposed to be made to work and remained in command of their soldiers in captivity.

Allied prisoners of war and their Japanese captors.

POET'S CORNER

A British army officer, Michael Riviere was taken prisoner by the Germans in Crete in 1941. He twice escaped from prison camps in Germany, but was recaptured each time. Finally he was sent to Colditz, from which escape was supposed to be impossible. He was freed at the end of the war.

German and Italian prisoners of war working on the roads in Scotland.

But these rules were not always followed. The Germans allowed millions of Russian prisoners to starve to death, and few German prisoners survived captivity in Russia. The Japanese had a special contempt for prisoners, since they believed that surrender was dishonourable. Large numbers of British, American and Commonwealth servicemen died in Japanese POW camps.

Unseen Fire

R.N. Currey (1907–)

❁

This is a damned inhuman sort of war.
I have been fighting in a dressing-gown
Most of the night; I cannot see the guns,
The sweating gun-detachments or the planes;

❁

I sweat down here before a symbol thrown
Upon a screen, sift facts, initiate
Swift calculations and swift orders; wait
For the precise split-second to order fire.

❁

We chant our ritual words; beyond the phones
A ghost repeats the orders to the guns:
One Fire... Two Fire... ghosts answer: the guns
roar
Abruptly; and an aircraft waging war
Inhumanly from nearly five miles height
Meets our bouquet of death — and turns sharp
right.
(c. 1942)

gun-detachments
The crew who fire the guns.

bouquet of death
The explosion of the gunfire.

The poet is in an anti-aircraft command post, following the path of enemy aircraft on a radar screen and giving orders to a gun crew. He has been woken from sleep by the air raid – that is why he is in his dressing-gown. It seems 'inhuman' to him because he is fighting against people he can't even see. Even the men firing the anti-aircraft guns seem so remote they are unreal – like ghosts. The aircraft is also fighting 'inhumanly' because its crew can't see the victims of their bombs. The plane takes evasive action and the anti-aircraft fire misses its target.

A painting of a radar station on the British coast in 1940.

POET'S CORNER

R.N. Currey was born in South Africa. He was drafted into anti-aircraft artillery, and developed an obsession with this war of machines, in which you might kill a person without ever seeing them. He worried that by making war impersonal, modern technology made killing too easy. He wrote: 'A man who is too squeamish to kill a rabbit can launch a rocket'.

Throughout the war, scientists worked to develop better weapons systems. One of the most important developments was radar. Invented by the British before the war, it improved until planes were able to fight at night and guns to fire at unseen targets tracked on a screen. Jet engines were another pre-war invention that came into use in wartime. Both the Germans and the British had jet fighters by the end of the war, with the potential to travel faster than any aircraft had done before.

The Germans developed pilotless aircraft, the V1s or 'doodlebugs'. These flew until they ran out of fuel and then fell to the ground. Packed with explosives, they did a lot of damage around London. Later came the V2s, rockets which travelled faster than sound, hitting their targets without warning. Although they were too inaccurate to do much harm, they were the ancestors of the rockets used to explore outer space.

A German V2 rocket taking off.

A little girl has lost her mother, killed when the atomic bomb was dropped on the Japanese city of Hiroshima in August 1945. Every month she visits the temple where there is a memorial to her mother, and where her mother's spirit is supposed to live on. The girl imagines that her mother can see her – but she cannot see her mother. She is distressed to think that she can no longer remember her clearly. The bomb dropped on Hiroshima killed at least 70,000 people.

Every Month: The Ten-Year-Old Girl

Marc Kaminsky (1943–)

❀

My house
was close to the place where the bomb fell

❀

My mother
was turned to white bone before
the family altar

❀

Grandfather and I
go to visit her on the sixth of every month

❀

Mother
is now living in the temple at Nakajima

❀

Mother
must be so pleased
to see how big I've gotten

❀

but all I see
is the Memorial Panel quietly standing there
no matter how I try
I can't remember what Mother looks like

(c.1984)

the bomb
The atom bomb dropped on Hiroshima.

family altar
Japanese families had an altar for worship in their homes.

Memorial Panel
A panel put up in memory of the girl's mother.

The war got more and more destructive as it went on. British and American bomber aircraft devastated German and Japanese cities, causing death and destruction on a far larger scale than Britain had suffered in the Blitz. In one raid on the German city of Dresden in February 1945, more than 25,000 people were killed.

The crew of the Enola Gay, *which dropped the first atomic bomb on Hiroshima on 6 August 1945.*

The devastation of Nagasaki after the atomic bomb was dropped by the United States on 9 August 1945.

POET'S CORNER

Marc Kaminsky is an American writer and therapist. He has been deeply interested in what young and old people have to say about their experiences of life. This poem is based on the experience of a Japanese girl, Sachiko Habu.

After Germany surrendered in May 1945, the war against Japan continued. The peak of destruction was reached when atom bombs were dropped on the Japanese cities of Hiroshima and Nagasaki in August 1945. Scientists working in the United States had taken four years to develop the atom bomb. A single bomb was capable of destroying an entire city. It also released a large amount of deadly nuclear radiation. The Japanese surrendered soon after the atom bombs were dropped, ending the war.

GLOSSARY

Difficult words from the verse appear alongside each poem. This glossary explains words used in the main text. The page numbers are given so that you can study the glossary and then see how the words have been used.

Allied (pp. 23, 25) The Allies were the countries fighting against Germany, Italy, and Japan – chiefly Britain, the USA and the Soviet Union. Their soldiers were called the Allied forces. Their opponents were known as the Axis forces.

atomic bomb (pp. 28, 29) An atomic bomb, or atom bomb, was a bomb that released nuclear energy to create a far bigger explosion than could ever be achieved with normal explosives.

baptism of fire (p. 21) The first time a soldier goes into battle is called his 'baptism of fire'.

Blitz (pp. 7, 29) The Blitz was the bombing of British cities by German aircraft in World War II.

blackout (p. 7) In Britain's towns and cities during World War II all streetlights were switched off and people had to carefully cover their windows with thick material before turning the lights on in their homes. This was called the blackout. It made it more difficult for enemy aircraft to find the targets they wanted to bomb.

captor (pp. 24, 25) Someone who is holding another person prisoner.

chivalry (p. 15) Treating your enemies in war with respect as honourable and worthy opponents.

Commonwealth (p. 15) Group of countries, once ruled by Britain as part of its worldwide empire, which chose to keep up links after becoming independent. Commonwealth troops from Canada, Australia, New Zealand and South Africa played a large part in World War II, as did soldiers from countries that were then still part of the British Empire, such as India and the West Indies.

communist (p. 19) During World War II the Soviet Union was ruled by a single political party, the Communist Party.

conscripts (p. 4) Men and women who have to join the armed forces whether they like it or not.

convoy (p. 17) A group of merchant ships that sail together, protected from attack by warships.

dictator (pp. 13, 19) An individual who rules a country as they like, without respect for freedom or laws. Three dictators led major countries in World War II: Adolf Hitler in Germany, Joseph Stalin in the Soviet Union, and Benito Mussolini in Italy.

evacuation (p. 11) Scheme for sending people, especially children, away from areas that were likely to be bombed. People who had been evacuated were known as 'evacuees'.

evasive action (p. 26) Dodging from side to side to avoid being hit.

exile (p. 19) When people have been forced to leave their home country to live abroad, they are said to be 'in exile'.

gas-masks (p. 11) At the start of World War II, Britain expected the Germans to use poison gas against British cities. People were given gas-masks to protect them against such an attack – which, in fact, never happened.

ghetto (p. 12) Under Nazi rule, Jews were cut off from the rest of the population and forced to live in separate parts of towns or cities called ghettos. Nowadays, the word 'ghetto' is often used to mean any overcrowded city district where only poor people live.

Holocaust (p. 13) 'Holocaust' means 'great destruction or loss of life'. It is especially used to refer to the mass murder of Jews by the Nazis during World War II.

impersonal (p. 27) *Without human feeling or emotional involvement.*

infantry (pp.19, 21) *Soldiers who fight on foot with light weapons such as rifles.*

Land Army (p. 9) *The Women's Land Army provided women — known as 'land girls' — to work on farms or in forestry during the war.*

merchant ship (p. 17) *A ship used to carry goods such as food or machines — as opposed to a naval ship or warship, used for fighting.*

munitions factory (pp. 7, 9) *A factory in which bullets, artillery shells or bombs are made.*

Nazi (pp. 12, 13) *A member or supporter of the Nazi Party, which ruled Germany during the war.*

nervous breakdown (p. 21) *A person who has a nervous breakdown becomes depressed, anxious and permanently tired, usually after some particularly stressful experience.*

night-shift (p. 8) *Working shifts, with one group of workers taking over from another in the course of the day and night, is a way of keeping factories operating for very long hours.*

nuclear radiation (p. 29) *An invisible, harmful result of an atomic explosion.*

prisoner of war (pp. 24, 25) *A soldier, sailor or airman captured by the enemy.*

radar (pp. 26, 27) *A means of tracking aircraft or ships — they show up as blips on a screen.*

rationing (p. 11) *A system introduced by the government during the war to ensure that scarce essential items such as food and clothing were fairly shared out. Each person was either allowed a precise amount of a particular thing — say, 8 ounces (220 grams) of jam a month — or given 'points' to spend as they chose. Your clothing points, for example, could be used to get two shirts or one pair of trousers, as you preferred.*

resistance movement (p. 13) *Secret organisation set up to resist Nazi rule in a country occupied by the Germans.*

Slavs (p. 19) *Many of the people of central and eastern Europe are Slavs. They include the Russians, Poles, Ukrainians and Czechs.*

Books to Read

For younger readers

Eyewitness: World War II by Simon Adams (DK Publishing, 2000)

Germany and Japan Attack by Sean Sheehan (Hodder Wayland, 2000)

Great Battles of World War II by Ole Steen Hansen (Hodder Wayland, 2000)

Leaders of World War II by Stewart Ross (Hodder Wayland, 2000)

My Secret Camera: Life in the Lodz Ghetto by Mendel Grossman and Frank Dabba Smith (Gulliver Books, 2000)

Poetry of the Second World War by Desmond Graham (ed.) (Pimlico, 1998)

World War II: The Allied Victory by Sean Sheehan (Hodder Wayland, 2000)

For older readers

Children in the Holocaust and World War II: Their Secret Diaries, by Laurel Holliday (ed.) (Washington Square Press, 1996)

The Second World War in Colour by Stewart Binns and Adrian Wood (Imperial War Museum, 2000)

The Terrible Rain: The War Poets 1939–45 by Brian Gardner (ed.) (Methuen, 1999)

INDEX

Numbers in **bold** refer to pictures and captions.